MW01165325

THE LAST SPIRIT OF FALL BROOK

Shirley M. Welch

Shirley M. Welch 6-15-2024

1

Copyright 2024 by Shirley M. Welch

All rights are reserved. No part of this book may be reproduced or transmitted in any form by any means, electronic, mechanical, magnetic, photographic, including photocopying, recording, or by any information or retrieval system without prior written permission of the publisher.

The stories in this book are based on the history and folklore associated with Fall Brook, Pennsylvania, a mining town that no longer exists in Tioga County. The author adds her own impressions of the ghostly area marked mainly by a crumbling graveyard.

The Last Spirit of Fall Brook is dedicated to my mother, **Dorotha Cleveland** (1936-2024).

Published by BookBaby
www.bookbaby.com

CONTENTS

CREDITS

Many thanks to these helpful folks and reliable history sources:

Author, William P. Robertson, for editing and formatting this book

Fall Brook California Historical Society and historian, Tom Frew, for permission to use Fall Brook photos from their collection

Pamela Mahonski Rayburn for snapping the cover photograph

John Tanner for taking the pic of the old Welch farmhouse

David Cox for designing the stylish cover

The *Steuben Farmers' Advocate* newspaper

The Wellsboro Herald newspaper

History Center, Mansfield, Pennsylvania

Joyce M. Tice's Tri-Counties Genealogy & History Website

Microsoft Bing

Fallbrookrailway.com

Blossburg Coal Center for permission to use their Fall Brook map on this page

Other photos by Shirley M. Welch, Dee Dee Ostrom, Bob Burns, and William P. Robertson

The Fall Brook pictures on pages 21 and 37 created by Shirley M. Welch

The locomotive and coal mining engravings on pages 23 and 30 are from the John Magee monument located in the Village Green at Wellsboro, Pennsylvania

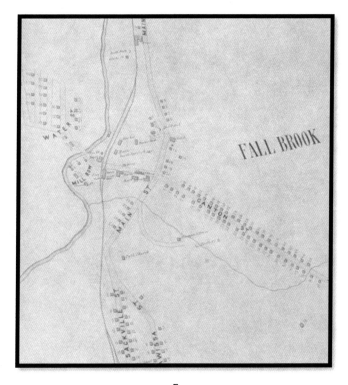

FALL BROOK CEMETERY POEM

In 1865, the *Steuben Farmers' Advocate* published a poem written by a former resident of Fall Brook who had moved away after the coal mines closed. The poem was titled "Fall Brook Cemetery," and it expressed the poet's nostalgic sadness for the town and its people. The person's name has been lost through time, but the poem remains:

I wander through the silent graves
where sleep the dead of Fall Brook town.
The grass was green, the flowers fair, the birds
sang sweetly all around.
I read the names of those I knew,
who lived in days of yore.
The old, the young, the rich, the poor,
are gone to come no more.

I thought of all the joys and woes,
the hopes, the fears, the smiles, and tears
that filled their lives in Fall Brook town.
I thought how busy was the place
that once was full of life and sound
is now a spot where ghosts abound.
I sighed and turned away, and said,
"Farewell, ye graves, where sleep the dead
of silent Fall Brook town."

CHAPTER 1: FIRST VISIT

The first time I visited Fall Brook I felt an eerie chill pass through me. It was not due to the cold wind that shook the trees or the snow that covered the ground. It was something else. Something I couldn't explain. I had come here to visit the souls who had left their homeland to work the coal mines of Tioga County. I had heard how Fall Brook was once a thriving town. How it had a railroad, a school, a church, and a cemetery. How it was the source of a superior coal that was in high demand for many industries. Other stories told how the coal ran out, the people left, and the town was abandoned and forgotten. I did not expect to experience the ardent emotions that invaded my being when I came here.

As I walked along the road that led to the town, I saw remnants of the past. In my mind, I envisioned the rusty Fall Brook Coal Company sign, the bridge that crossed Fall Brook Creek, and the stone wall that marked the entrance to the cemetery. I felt a strange connection to this place as if I could hear the voices of the people who had lived here, who had worked here, and who had died here. I wondered if they were happy, or if they longed for their homes across the sea. I wondered if they knew that their town would be no more and that their descendants would forget them.

I decided to explore the area, hoping to find some undiscovered history. I had a hand-drawn map that pinpointed the church, the school, the general store, the post office, the coal chutes, the horse barns, the hotel, and the cemetery. I found my way to the graveyard by walking the path where many others had trod. It was a serene place surrounded by trees and was on a hill that once overlooked the village. The cemetery is overgrown now and very hard to locate.

Wandering among the graves, I looked for the ones that matched my list by reading the names and dates etched on the tombstones. I saw many familiar names that I had seen in records and the newspapers I had researched. I found the resting place of those born in Scotland, England, Wales, Ireland, Germany, Poland, and many local villages. Some had died from accidents, diseases, or suicide. Others succumbed to natural causes or from unknown reasons. Most had been buried with their families. The rest were interred with friends or with no one at all. I saw names of people who had left a mark on Fall Brook's history resting side-by-side with those who had faded into obscurity.

I finally found the grave of Robert and Annie Russell near the front of the cemetery. They had a simple headstone inscribed with their names and the dates and places of birth and death. Robert Russell was born on April 12, 1834 in Cumbernauld, Scotland. He died on November 12, 1905. Annie was born on March 7, 1837 in the same town as her husband and died on May 4, 1870. They had been married for many years and had lived in Fall Brook for most of them. They had worked in the mines, raised their children, and attended church. They had been loyal and faithful to each other and to their community. Robert was treasurer of the Friendly Society of Fall Brook. He was trustworthy, reliable, and supportive of the town.

A sudden surge of emotion swept over me as I stood before the Russells' grave. I felt a sense of gratitude for their courage and sacrifice and a sense of pride for their strength and resilience. I was overwhelmed by love as I pondered their character and spirit.

I knelt and touched their grave marker. As I traced the engravings on the cold stone, I felt a warmth that contrasted with the frigid air. I whispered a prayer, thanking them for their lives and asking for their blessing. My prayer was answered by a breeze that seemed to welcome me home. I smiled and felt a peace I had never experienced before.

I stayed there for a while to talk to the Russells. I told them about my family and my life. I said that I had come to Fall Brook to learn more about them and to honor them. I had come to learn more about myself, too. I had a feeling that Fall Brook had something to teach me.

"I believe that Fall Brook has a spirit and a soul," I mumbled as the breeze blew my words into the surrounding forest. Then I rose to leave after telling the ghosts they should not follow me home.

I did not know it then, but I was right. Fall Brook does have a lingering soul that was waiting to reveal itself to me and share its history seeped in tragedy and glory. Told by the Last Spirit of Fall Brook, this book shares a Pennsylvania ghost town's legacy.

CHAPTER 2: HISTORY OF FALL BROOK

In 1857, Duncan Magee discovered a large vein of semi-bituminous coal near Fall Brook Creek in Tioga County Pennsylvania. His father, John, then purchased 6,000 acres of land from C.I. Ward of Towanda and mining operations were begun with drift No. 1 dug into the mountainside. After enduring immense political pressure exerted by rival concerns, the Fall Brook Coal Company was chartered on April 7, 1859.

In 1858, John Magee also founded Fall Brook town that grew to 1,400 residents by 1862. At its zenith, there were 180 dwellings sprawled along the mountain. They included a schoolhouse, three boarding houses, a saw mill, two carpenter shops, three weighing offices, and two blacksmith shops. The Fall Brook Coal Company was the main employer and ran a company store to accommodate the miners it hired. The town was incorporated in 1864.

By 1865, Fall Brook saw still more improvements. A grand hotel opened that year with Warren Goff named as its first manager. The railroad depot was finished, too, after the telegraph line from Corning was completed the previous fall. In 1869, the Alba and Fall Brook stage line provided another means of travel from the tidy little town.

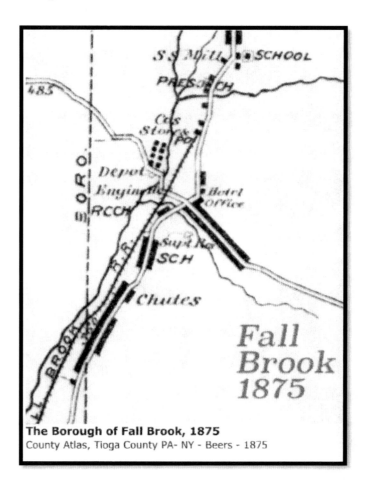

The Borough of Fall Brook, 1875
County Atlas, Tioga County PA- NY - Beers - 1875

To sustain their new village and haul their coal to market, the Magees established the Fall Brook Railway in 1859. It ran a little over six miles as a spur line to the Tioga Railroad at Blossburg, Pennsylvania. From there, the coal was shipped to Corning, New York and on to the Erie Canal. Their product was in high demand because of its superior quality. It was ideal for blacksmithing, glass making, and furnace use.

Life in Fall Brook, though, was hard and dangerous for the miners. It was backbreaking work as they gouged in the earth with picks and shovels. They had to work long hours in the dark and dusty tunnels, facing the risk of accidents, cave-ins, and explosions. They also suffered from black lung disease and eye infections from the coal dust. The miners were paid by the tons of coal they harvested, which varied depending on the quality and quantity. They also had to pay for their own tools, equipment, and supplies.

Women and children played a role in coal mining, too. They worked alongside the men doing various tasks, such as digging, hauling, sorting, and cleaning coal. They pushed or pulled heavy tubs and often crawled on their hands and knees in narrow passages. Young children were given the job of opening and closing doors.

Other disasters made life more difficult, as well. Fall Brook was the victim of a smallpox outbreak in the winter of 1871 that claimed the lives of many youngsters. Then the following May, a wildfire swept through the surrounding woods. It would have engulfed the village if the entire population hadn't pitched in to fight it.

Miners lived in crowded houses owned and controlled by the coal company. In 1887, there were 250 such tenements. The houses were drafty and built of wood. They had no indoor plumbing or electricity. That gave the families a strong sense of community, and they supported each other in times of need and hardship.

The coal chutes in Fall Brook, Pennsylvania in the late 1860s are pictured above. The Fall Brook Hotel can be seen in the left-hand corner near the skyline. One can imagine stepping out of the magnificent hotel and hearing the noise from all the mining activity.

Fall Brook continued to thrive while two hundred thousand tons of coal were harvested annually over a three decade period. By the 1890s, however, production was slowed by the depletion of the veins and regional competition. Then, in 1892, the coal and railroad operations were split into two separate companies when business got bad.

The August 25, 1897 edition of the *Mansfield Advertiser* reported the inevitable end, as follows: "We are informed that the coal at Fall

Brook is not expected to hold out more than eighteen months longer, and that as soon as the supply of timber in that vicinity has become exhausted, the railroad will be taken up. Fall Brook will then become a veritable deserted village." According to the *Wellsboro Agitator* this actually occurred on August 18, 1899 when the town's miners laid down their tools for good.

CHAPTER 3: JOHN MAGEE

John Magee was a man of remarkable achievements. Born in 1794 near Easton, Pennsylvania, he distinguished himself during the War of 1812, when as a courier for General Hull at Detroit, he twice delivered messages on horseback to Washington while being fired upon by the enemy. After the war, he arrived penniless in Steuben County, New York. During his first winter there, he worked for eight dollars a month until he earned enough to buy a herd of cattle. He displayed his business sense by slaughtering them and selling their meat door-to-door.

Magee's first break came in 1818 when he was appointed constable of Bath, New York. He soon became county sheriff and then established stage coach lines to carry U.S. mail. In 1826, he was elected to Congress on the Democratic ticket and served two terms in the U.S. House of Representatives.

In the 1830s, Magee branched out into railroading and was instrumental in building the New York and Erie Railroad that connected the Hudson River to Lake Erie. He also helped construct the Bath and Hammondsport line and by 1854 owned the Blossburg and Corning Railway.

John began dabbling in coal mining, as well. In 1851, he leased mines in Blossburg, Pennsylvania while sending his son, Duncan, to explore for coal in the surrounding region. This resulted in the formation of the Fall Brook Coal Company. At that point, he moved from Bath to Watkins, New York to be closer to his mining operations. There, he bought enough property to build a trestle works and to handle large coal shipments. He also erected homes for himself and his workers.

In 1867, John Magee was selected as a delegate to the Constitutional Convention of the State of New York. As a millionaire, he now had investments in the Steuben County Bank, the Bath Gas and Light Company, the Green Bay and Mississippi Improvement Company, and many railroads.

On April 5, 1868, at the age of seventy-four, the entrepreneur died at home after inflicted by a paralysis attack two weeks before. He was a much beloved man, and according to the *Corning Journal*, many traveled from Pennsylvania to bid him adieu: "The large number of employees and officers of the Fall Brook Co., wore crepe badges on the arm, and marched two by two from the cars to the late residence of Mr. Magee, to see his face for the last time...this was a touching and appropriate tribute of respect for one who as an employer had the faculty of inspiring respect and enduring friendship."

Ironically, John Magee's funeral was the first service held in the Watkins' Presbyterian Church that he contributed $30,000 to help build. His outstanding character later resulted in an 1886 monument being erected in his memory on the Wellsboro, Pennsylvania Village Green. It bears a plaque that says: "The story of a useful and honored life may be told in these words. His energy and diligence compelled success. His ability and integrity won public confidence. His kindness and liberality drew to him the affectionate regard of rich and poor."

CHAPTER 4: FALL BROOK RAILWAY

It's hard to know what the train ride was like for the first passengers on the Fall Brook Railway in 1859, but it must have been a thrilling experience. As the engine chugged along the tracks, they would have felt the wind rushing through their hair and the sun shining down on their faces. The train was a symbol of progress and innovation. It opened new opportunities for the town to ship its coal, welcome new workers, and get essential supplies.

In December 1865, the depo was finished after carpenters had toiled for many weeks. As they proudly installed the Fall Brook, Pennsylvania sign, others made sure that the building clock worked. Every detail was important, for soon passengers would arrive for a very historic day in Fall Brook.

The ladies dressed in their finest attire. Their hats were pinned on properly and their high-top shoes laced tightly around their ankles. The men wore freshly pressed suits with their watch chains glinting in the sunlight. Awaiting the first visitors to the depot was a momentous occasion. Possibly, they brought news from the city or the newest fashion or fabric for the general store.

The passenger cars on the Fall Brook Railway were comfortable, with plush seats and large windows that offered panoramic views of the surrounding countryside. The train would have run at a leisurely pace, allowing the passengers to take in the sights and sounds of the journey. Travelers to the town would have seen the beautiful countryside from Blossburg and marveled at the rolling hills and lush green forest. As they neared the station, they'd have heard the whistle signaling their arrival and the excited chatter of those ready to disembark.

Most visitors who came to Fall Brook stayed at the grand hotel built by John Magee. As already noted, he was founder and president of the Fall Brook Coal Company and Fall Brook Railway. John constructed the lodge in 1865 as a showcase of his success and as a place to entertain his business associates and friends.

Yes, and Fall Brook Railway brought many famous people to the village, with Mark Twain being one of the first to arrive. Twain was an American humorist, journalist, and author noted for his travel narratives. He wrote a letter to his wife from Fall Brook on October 15, 1871. He described the town as a rough, wild place. He said it was situated in a valley walled in on both sides with picturesque hills. According to Mark, it had a great coal breaker, and the crashing machinery was heard whenever he stepped outdoors.

Later, Twain stopped by Fall Brook in 1885 on his way to his summer home in Elmira, New York. He was invited to stay at the Fall Brook Hotel by John Magee's son, Duncan, who was an admirer of the author's work. The celebrity was a big hit when he entertained the other guests with his witty stories and cunundrums.

Mark Twain's brother, Orion Clemons, actually lived in Fall Brook from 1871to 1873. He worked as a clerk for the Fall Brook Coal Company. He also wrote a weekly column for the local newspaper, *The Tioga County Agitator*. He hoped to establish himself as a lawyer in Pennsylvania but moved to Iowa when he failed.

Horace Greeley, editor of the *New-York Tribune* and a prominent politician, visited Fall Brook in 1868 during his presidential campaign. Then, in 1872, President U. S. Grant arrived in town, as well. He stayed at the hotel while returning from a fishing trip.

Other famous folks to stop by the village included Thomas A. Edison, inventor of the light bulb, phonograph, and many other devices. He visited in 1880 to inspect the coal mines and test his electric lamps. He stayed for several days and demonstrated his inventions to the awed guests and locals.

John Phillip Sousa, conductor of the famous Sousa Band, came via rail in 1899. He loved the village so much that he composed a march called "The Fall Brook Polka." He dedicated the song to the people of Fall Brook and the miners who worked there. It was a cheerful piece that featured clarinets, trumpets, trombones, tubas, and drums. Band members sang along to show how smitten they had become with the coal and railroad town.

CHAPTER 5: FALL BROOK HOTEL

Haunted by images of the Fall Brook Hotel, one must wonder what energy still exists in the place it stood. If it were still there today, what stories would it tell? Of course, this is just speculation based on limited information. One can only imagine the inn perched solidly on the mountainside, overlooking all that was happening below.

The Fall Brook Hotel was known for being a luxury establishment that catered to wealthy guests. The massive building had nearly 100 rooms that could accommodate up to 200 people. It was popular with businessmen, travelers, and tourists who came to see the nearby waterfalls and scenery. It was also a regular destination for rich sportsmen looking to bag deer or catch trout.

The hotel was constructed by John Magee. Its imposing architecture reflected the strong character of its owner. The three-story building had a front façade and a central entranceway that shouted, "Welcome." Its second and third floor balconies featured stout ornamental posts, too. Magee had built the establishment to impress his business associates and a continuous stream of famous people who made their way to Fall Brook. It also was the scene of many social events, weddings, parties, and celebrations.

The hotel was considered the finest eatery in the region due to its huge dining room and exquisite cuisine. One can imagine that the serving plates were likely made of ceramic or glass with a simple but elegant design. They might have contained the name or initials of the hotel or maybe a symbol related to coal mining. They would have been white or light-colored to contrast with the rich food. They'd also have been large enough to hold generous portions of meat, vegetables, and desserts.

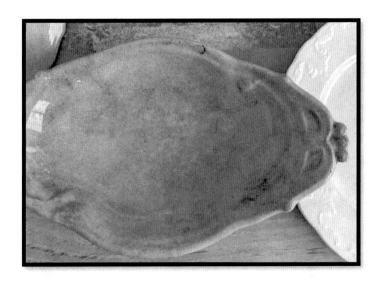

The hotel's glory days lasted until the mines ran dry in 1899. Then it was closed and left to decay along with the rest of the town. The night watchman was the only one on duty when a fire broke out and burned the inn to the ground. The place where Mark Twain's laughter had loudly rung and Thomas Edison had amazed folks with his ingenuity was sadly reduced to a pile of ashes by daybreak.

CHAPTER 6: HORSES OF FALL BROOK

Long gone are the horses of Fall Brook and the wagons that traveled through the once bustling town. There is no longer the pomp and circumstance of the steeds' thundering hooves as they pranced along the streets over one hundred years ago when such men as John Magee drew reins over them.

In 1873, carriages were a common sight as they carted visitors to and from town. The *Steuben Farmers' Advocate* reported that a new stable had been built in Fall Brook that same year by Mr. John Smith, who had recently moved from New York. The stable was said to be "one of the finest in the country" and could accommodate twenty horses. The newspaper also mentioned that Mr. Smith had a fine collection of horses, some of which he had brought with him and others he had purchased from local farmers.

In 1880, the same paper published a story about a horse race that took place in Fall Brook between two famous trotters named Frank and Nellie. The event was attended by a large crowd of spectators, who cheered and bet on their favorite competitor. The race was described as "a close and exciting contest" that Frank won by a neck in a time of two minutes and forty seconds.

In 1891, the *Farmers' Advocate* announced that a new blacksmith shop had been opened by Mr. James Brown, who had learned the trade from his father in England. Mr. Brown was praised as "a skillful and experienced workman" capable of shoeing horses, repairing wagons, making tools, and forging iron.

The newspaper reported in 1877 that an invention had been introduced in the Fall Brook mines, called the "horsepower hoisting machine." This device was designed to lift coal from the bottom of the shafts to the surface using the strength of two horses. It was "a great improvement over the old method of hoisting by hand" and saved much time and labor.

Then, in 1883, a news story was written about a remarkable horse named Dick, who worked in the Fall Brook mines for fifteen years. Dick was described as "a faithful and intelligent animal, who knew his duty and performed it well." Reportedly, Dick was "a great favorite with the miners, who treated him kindly and gave him many a lump of sugar or an apple." He and his stablemates were put out to pasture that same year by the Fall Brook Coal Company.

CHAPTER 7: TRAVELING TO FALL BROOK

In the late 1800s, the world moved at a much gentler pace. The journey from other towns to Fall Brook was no dash but a measured dance with time and terrain. Not everyone took the railroad. There were plenty of horse-drawn vehicles and foot traffic, too, traveling the dirt roads that connected the village to other parts of Tioga County.

From Wellsboro, the distance stretched twenty long miles. Horse-drawn buggies that set forth at dawn chose patience for a companion as their wheels creaked and groaned along the way. It wasn't until the sun sank behind Welch Mountain that the outskirts of their destination appeared at the end of an exhausting uphill pull. The crack of whips was often needed to spur their team of weary animals onto the streets ahead.

Those who drove by wagon from Mansfield rumbled along for twelve miles on a rough byway. The clip-clop of hooves accompanied them every step of the way while the forest stood sentinel on the knolls around them. In the summer months, travelers wore rough handkerchiefs around their faces to keep from eating dust. A rainstorm, on the other hand, could slow their progress to a muddy crawl.

A small footpath ran from Morris Run through Blossburg and Covington that led to Fall Brook. This was often used by miners on their way to work. Some of these hardy souls lived in company-owned homes that required them to walk quite a distance back and forth. Other miners, humming jaunty songs, took the same route from Arnot to visit friends and family. Eventually, a stagecoach ran from Arnot, as well.

Travelers from Blossburg were the lucky ones. They could ride the Fall Brook Railway six miles to town in a fraction of the time other visitors took to get there. When they alighted at the train depot in late afternoon, they didn't have dust on *their* boots!

Peddlers often made their way up Welch Mountain, too, with their wagons crammed with jingling merchandise. The pushier, disreputable ones were rumored to have disappeared along the way. Were they buried in farmhouse basements like the old wives whispered? Or was the gossip meant to keep such salesmen away?

CHAPTER 8: STROLL THROUGH TOWN

I imagine what life was like in Fall Brook in the 1800s whenever I walk down old Main Street, which is now known as Welch Mountain Road. I can only imagine stepping from my home and turning toward the general store to see what mail arrived on yesterday's train and what news is there from relatives or far-off friends. I can almost see the children playing near the school and merchants selling goods at the company store. The wind brings the sound of coal cars running on the railroad tracks and the whistle of the steam engine.

I greet everyone I meet with a friendly nod or smile. I say, "Good morning" or "Good afternoon," depending upon the time of day. I use formal titles like mister, missus, or miss when addressing strangers or acquaintances and first names when talking to friends or relatives. I avoid using slang or profanity, because that was considered rude.

I imagine a young Irish man walking by. He's a miner on his way to work. He totes a lantern and wears a ragged coat and cap. When he speaks, the lad reveals a thick accent and cheerful demeanor. "Top of the morning," he blares. "What have ye heard of the weather? This looks a bit like me home in Ireland, the mountains so green and such."

Children & Teachers at the Fall Brook School

Then I see a middle-aged German woman who runs the boarding house. "Guten Tag," she says by way of greeting. "I have a room should you need one." She wears a modest dress, a bonnet, and an apron. She has a stern face and a strong voice. She has bread to bake, pies to make, or cookies if she finds the time.

The man who works as a blacksmith says, "Howdy!" While I pass him, he compliments me on my shoes. He wears a leather apron and a coarse pair of pants. He has much to do, for the horses need shod and many tools need repaired. His assistant is a grinning Afro-American who has a caring way with the horses.

Next, I see the laundry lady with her hair pulled up in a bun. She already has some wash on the line and good mountain air to dry the men's shirts quickly, so they'll have them for another day's work.

"Got my clothes cleaned, Annie?" I ask with a friendly wave. "Here are some more items to add to your pile."

Annie's place is located near the train station. Often, travelers will drop off their fancy duds to be aired and straightened before having their photo snapped beside the depot, a coal car, or the mine entrance.

The Fall Brook Hotel is another good source of business for Annie. Someone may need a torn skirt repaired or a button sewn on. She is always ready with her scissors and thread at hand. There is not much rest for this lovely lady whose laundry services are always in demand.

With a smile, I realize how Fall Brook has become a melting pot of immigrants and local people. They all now blend together, and their friendly greetings ring from one end of the town to the other.

CHAPTER 9: HUMPHRIES BREWER

And so, Humphries Brewer, your story unfurls—a tapestry woven with coal dust, cider, and the gift of shoes. The Fall Brook Coal Company, the railway, and your spirit of resilience are historical elements while the specifics of your passing and the gift of shoes are woven from imagination.

Humphries Brewer was born on February 28, 1817 in Box, Wiltshire, England and met his end on December 25, 1867 in Fall Brook. He was 50 years, 9 months, and 27 days old at the time of his passing. His life was marked by many significant contributions as a quarry master and tunnel builder. In 1862, he was made manager of the Fall Brook Coal Company and oversaw all its operations. A grave responsibility, indeed!

Upon Brewer's death, Duncan Magee, owner of the company, ordered all business to stop. Shops, offices, stores, and locomotives were draped in black mourning cloth as a token of respect. All of Fall Brook turned out for his funeral. Many traveled from far-off Corning to attend.

Humphries Brewer was more than a name etched on a tombstone. Under his watchful eye, the Fall Brook Coal Company breathed life into the hills. Let his voice echo across time along with the rhythm of pickaxes and the clatter of train wheels. Let it tell of the soot-streaked faces of the miners and the rugged terrain connecting Fall Brook to the world beyond.

A Gift Unwrapped

Let us imagine the atmosphere on that crisp Christmas Day in 1867 when Humphries Brewer breathed his last. The community of Fall Brook was adorned with festive decorations, the warmth of hearths, and the scent of pine. Families gathered around tables laden with hearty meals, sharing stories and laughter. The church bells rang, echoing through the snow-covered streets, inviting all to celebrate the birth of Christ.

Yet, amidst this joy, there was a sober note. Humphries Brewer, who had left his mark on the earth, now embarked on a different journey. His spirit, perhaps, lingered near the mine shafts he once oversaw. The hematoma that claimed his life was a silent adversary, a rupture within, much like the unseen veins of coal deep beneath the ground.

As the sun dipped below the mountains, casting long shadows, the townsfolk lit candles and exchanged gifts. The memory of Humphries Brewer was honored, too, as stories were shared of his dedication and his ability to guide miners through a vast labyrinth of tunnels. His grave nestled in Fall Brook Cemetery became a silent witness to the passage of time.

And so, on that Christmas Day, there was a blend of celebration and mourning, of memories and hope. Humphries Brewer's legacy, etched in stone and whispered by the wind, became part of a season of love, loss, and the quiet resilience of the human spirit.

Casting shadows upon Fall Brook Cemetery, Humphries Brewer rests well, and his story lives on. His spirit, like a miner's lamp flickering in the dark, guides us towards the depth of memory. His memory endures, entwined with the frost-kissed air of that Christmas Day— a day when both joy and sorrow danced upon the snow-covered streets of Fall Brook.

Believe or doubt, as your heart dictates, for ghosts, like memories, are elusive. They slip through our fingers, leaving behind whispers and questions. And perhaps, Humphries Brewer's spirit found solace in sharing its truth as a moment in time across the veil. Listen. The wind may carry his voice once more, weaving the past into the present like the delicate strands of a spider web, catching moonlight and memory.

He speaks of a hematoma—a rupture, a farewell. His death records, once filed away, now flutter like moth wings. The veil thins, and he imparts his tale. You become the keeper of his secret, the bridge between realms. His words, like moonbeams, melt upon your mind.

He speaks of the shoes that arrived on that fateful Christmas Day, December 25, 1867. And then, as if by fate, a knock echoes through the house. The door creaks open, revealing a figure swathed in winter's embrace. A neighbor holds a package, wrapped in brown paper and tied by twine. "From the heart of Fall Brook," the neighbor says, placing the parcel in his trembling hands. "A Christmas Gift."

Humphries Brewer smiles as he unwraps the package. He spots a pair of study shoes, their leather supple and the soles unmarred. They bear witness to the footsteps of countless miners— their dreams and burdens absorbed into the fibers. He slips them on, and they cradle his weary feet. They symbolize the warmth of the community, of its shared struggle.

The Final Journey for Humphries Brewer

As the snowflakes pirouette outside, he rises from his chair. The shoes carry him across the creaking floorboards, out into the moon-kissed night. The cemetery awaits with its silent congregation of souls. He treads lightly, as if not to disturb his slumbering ancestors.

And there, beneath the snow-draped boughs, he finds his resting place. The gravestone bears his name, chiseled with care. The hematoma's echo fades, replaced by the whisper of snowflakes. He lies down, his breath mingling with the frost.

"Merry Christmas, Fall Brook," he murmurs, closing his eyes.

The Wellsboro Herald noted Humphries Brewer's passing, as follows: "It is with a melancholy feeling that we announce the death of Humphries Brewer. We cannot suffer the occasion to pass without passing some feeble tribute to the memory of one who was endeared to almost every person."

CHAPTER 10: TOWN PHOTOGRAPHER

Photographer, John Tanner, was a dreamer whose heartbeat was in rhythm with his camera shutter. He knew that photography was more than just capturing light. It was about weaving stories. Fall Brook became John's canvas, and the faces of its people held secrets to be revealed.

John wandered the streets, chasing the elusive magic of everyday life amid the miners and storekeepers. He recorded the seasons, the festivals, the weddings, the funerals, and the laughing children. Yet, success still seemed to elude him.

Because John wanted to make a career of photography, he worked in a Mansfield studio for a while to hone his craft. Then he moved back to Fall Brook and set up his own business. At first, his prospects looked bright, but after a year, he found it a poor way to make a living. Crayon portraits were stylish in the 1800s, so he did quite a few of those. Sadly, his prices were too high for most of his customers. He later tried his hand at charcoal portraits that were photos enhanced by artists. They, too, didn't sell.

John photographed family members at the farmhouse at the bottom of the mountain. He sought out the people of Fall Brook, including the wrinkled farmer, the baker kneading bread, and the teacher with a secret smile. He wanted to record all their stories, but the townsfolk weren't impressed with his work. Although he wasn't a great success in the eyes of the world, he had captured something deeper—the heartbeat of the village.

Tanner realized that dreams weren't measured in fame or fortune. They bloomed in the hearts of those who see the unseen. Be it in a book or a photo, John knew the importance of preserving the history of his chosen land and people.

So, John Tanner's legacy lives on in the shadows of Fall Brook. His artistic passion still lingers in the air. His 1933 death did not separate him from the mountain he loves. Through his photos, he appears as a glimpse from the past in the ever-enclosing darkness.

CHAPTER 11: THE WELCHES OF FALL BROOK

Halfway up the mountain toward Fall Brook lived Samuel Welch and his wife, Abbie, in a farmhouse they built with their own hands. They cleared the land, laid the rock foundation, and raised the sturdy frame. The scent of newly cut lumber from the local sawmill mingled with the promise of a new life.

Sam answered the call to duty when the American Civil War broke out. He enlisted in September of 1861 in Mainesburg, joining Company A of the New York Engineering Regiment as a private. In November of the same year, he was promoted to lieutenant and served as an artillery weapons mechanic. After being wounded at the Battle of Fredericksburg in December 1862, he was mustered out of service on September 20, 1864 at Elmira, New York.

While her husband was off fighting, Abbie kept the home fires burning and the farm going the best she could. She was overjoyed at Sam's return when her life became normal again. To celebrate, she bought a pair of peacocks from a peddler who passed their house. The feathers were very popular among the ladies who adorned their bonnets with them. Abbie made other money by picking berries and peppermint leaves that she sold in town. Her potatoes were also in great demand.

There were days when Sam's footsteps took him beyond the farm and on up the mountain. His destination was the general store that stood in the heart of Fall Brook, its creaky floors bearing the weight of countless transactions. A man of great stature, Sam entered as the bell above the door announced his arrival. The shopkeeper merely greeted him with a nod while Welch's eyes traveled over the shelves that held everything from flour to kerosene lamps.

Sam lingered near the counter listening to the latest news. The store was the hub of gossip and camaraderie. He bought a sack of coffee beans, a treat for his early mornings tending the horses in the barn. He then began searching for a particular relish dish his wife had set her sights on. This dish was made of ironstone, a durable type of pottery that resembled fine porcelain but was more affordable and practical.

"Unfortunately," the clerk told Sam, "them dishes is only found at the Fall Brook Hotel."

The problem was solved soon after, because Abbie raised the best chickens and supplied their large eggs to the hotel. On his very next delivery, Sam exchanged the eggs for two ironstone dishes that his wife totally adored!

The Welch lineage has continued within the walls of the clapboard farmhouse to this day with each generation leaving its mark. John Tanner took this photograph of the homestead along with the original family that dwelt there:

Samuel Welch, born April 1837, died January 25, 1924

Abbie M. Doyen Welch, born January 1843, died July 24, 1918

Eugene Welch, born February 14, 1875, died December 24, 1962

Emma Bell Tanner Welch, born July 24, 1876, died June 7, 1961

CHAPTER 12: FALL BROOK LEGENDS

The Witch of Fall Brook

In the heart of the dense Fall Brook woods, where the ancient trees stood, there lived a woman known as Evelyn Hawthorn. Evelyn's life unfolded in the late 1800s, a time when superstitions clung to the air like morning mist. Her cottage sat on the outskirts of Fall Brook where the forest murmured secrets to those who dared listen. Nestled amidst the wildflowers and moss-covered stones, her home was a haven for those who sought her skills.

Herbs were hung out to dry. Only Evelyn knew what they were for as she harvested them for healing. From the corn she grew, she also made the best brooms around. She used the long, beautiful stands of hair from her horse's tail to wrap the besoms and make them strong and lasting.

Her horse, grazing nearby, would stand for hours while Hawthorn brushed her long, flowing mane. A mare like no other, she warned Evelyn of unexpected visitors with a pawing of her foot. She would snort if danger was near and whinny when needed.

Evelyn was no ordinary woman. Her eyes held the wisdom of centuries, and her hands bore the calluses of countless nights tending to the sick and weary. She was a midwife, a healer, and a keeper of forgotten knowledge. But Evelyn's true power lie in her connection to the Fall Brook land.

She wandered the forest, her skirt brushing against ferns and dew-kissed petals.

The townsfolk whispered that she could mend broken bones with a touch and soothe fevered brows with her incantations. When sickness struck, and doctors' medicine failed, desperate families sought out the herb mistress. Faithfully, she emerged from her cottage to attend their every need. She delivered babies by candlelight. She brewed teas that banished nightmares and made salves that mended wounds. Fall Brook thrived under her watchful eye. She cured ailments and tended to the injured, the young, and the old. She never asked for anything in return except the promise: "Do me no harm."

But darkness has a way of harming even the purest of hearts. One bitter winter, a stranger arrived asking Evelyn to reveal her secrets. He believed her herbs held the key to eternal life. She was not about to divulge the knowledge entrusted to her by her dear mother. She refused every gift he offered.

"The earth yields its gifts willingly," she told the glaring man. "But it punishes greed!"

The stranger left her cottage in a rage to spread vengeful rumors. He swore Evelyn was a sorceress who stole souls until fear spread like wildfire through Fall Brook. The townsfolk, once grateful, now cast wary glances at her when she passed down the street. They blamed her for every misfortune, forgetting the lives she had saved. Finally, a torch-bearing mob descended upon the midwife's home to accuse her of witchcraft.

Evelyn stood defiant, her eyes aflame. "I'm no witch!" she spat. "I'm nature's vessel. Bound by ancient ways."

The crowd was torn between fear and awe. As Evelyn whispered a protective spell, the leaves swirled around her. Then the townsfolk spoke of her powers, attributing them to her lineage that traced back to the witches of old England. With a collective gasp, they backed away, cowed and fearful.

The Fall Brook Cemetery was Evelyn's sanctuary. She went there when the sun dipped below the horizon, casting long shadows over the tombstones. Her footsteps, light as a moth's wing, carried her through damp grass. She wore a cloak spun from moonlight and stars that made her appear ghost-like.

The townsfolk watched from behind the trees as she moved among the graves. Her fingers traced the names of those etched in stone, and she whispered incantations, words lost to time. The flowers that she carried were no ordinary blossoms but moonlight lilies, shadow roses, and graveyard violets. Each petal held a memory, a fragment, a life gone too soon.

Evelyn's purpose was clear; she tended to the souls laid to rest. When a fresh mound appeared, she knelt and dug her tiny fingers into the soil. She planted her spectral flowers, weaving magic into the earth. Then the ground trembled, and grateful whispers from the departed were heard.

The townspeople once again spoke of Evelyn in hushed tones. Some feared her while others sought her out in desperation. Mothers left offerings at her doorstep. She accepted their gifts: a lock of hair, a silver coin, a tear-stained letter.

To this day, if one wanders near the Fall Brook Cemetery, he might see some unusual flowers growing in a place he did not expect to find them. Yes, Evelyn still tends these blooms, as she could not cross the veil. Forever caught between worlds, her figure of mist and moonlight is often seen dancing amongst the graves.

The Stone Bridge of Fall Brook

In the heart of Fall Brook, where the forest meets the edge of town, there stands an ancient stone bridge. Its moss-covered stones hold its secret, and it remains a place where the veil between worlds grows thin. But as with all stone structures, it acquired a soul, a presence that lingered long after the masons had completed their work.

The townspeople spoke of strange occurrences near the bridge. On moonlit nights, they'd hear soft voices carried by the breeze, whispers that seem to rise from the very stones. Some claim it was the wind playing tricks, but others knew better. They knew the bridge held memories imprinted like footprints in mud.

One tale passed down through generations spoke of a forlorn lover. His name was William

Brown, who died by suicide in Fall Brook in 1896. He was a quiet young man of twenty-five and worked as a clerk for the coal company. He fell in love with the beautiful blacksmith's daughter, whose eyes were shimmering emeralds. She sang like an angel in church each Sunday until she totally captured his heart. They were careful, though, to keep their courtship away from prying eyes, for Sarah's father disapproved of her penniless beau. The only place they could safely meet was the stone bridge where the gurgling water hid their passionate vows.

One fateful evening, Brown waited at the bridge with his heart pounding madly. Sarah was late, and it seemed like an eternity before he heard her furtive footsteps. When she finally arrived, her green eyes were wide with fear. The blacksmith had learned of their affair and threatened to disown her. William begged Sarah to go away with him, but she dared not. Her father then sent her to a far-off city where she'd never see Brown again.

The young man suffered horribly from depression and financial woes. Being separated from his loving Sarah made life so unbearable that he shot himself in the face with a borrowed revolver. The local newspaper called Brown "a bright and promising young man, who had many friends and acquaintances in Fall Brook, and whose sad and untimely end cast a gloom over the entire community." The blacksmith showed no sign of remorse.

The stone bridge of Fall Brook, with its ancient stones and whispered secrets, still stands today as a witness to the heartbroken lovers. Travelers and locals alike cross over it on their way to the nearby waterfalls, and some hear murmurs not made by the wind. The eternal promise of William and Sarah continues to linger in the cool forest air to be heard by those attuned to their spirits.

The Lady in White

Names etched in faded letters that once belonged to the living are now claimed by the earth. But one grave stood apart—an unmarked one near the birch tree at the back of the grounds. As for the old birch, it bore scars where ropes once hung. Words engraved by those who fear no evil left an indelible mark on its bark. This tree is a symbol of life and the inevitability of death. Its white skin glowing in the moonlight is a sign of the tree's spectral nature.

Legend spoke of the Lady in White, her name forgotten and her face lost to time, who wandered Fall Brook graveyard at night. Her footsteps left no trace, yet her presence lingered— a soft sigh on the wind, a fleeting touch against paling cheeks.

Visitors reported hearing her weeping, a mournful melody that echoed through the moonlit tombstones. They saw her ethereal form clad in a tattered white gown. Her eyes were hollow and pleading. She beckoned to them. Her translucent fingers urged them closer. Those who obeyed were swallowed by the birch tree's shadow, not to be seen again. Later, their voices joined the chorus that forever emanates from the tombstones.

And so, on a moonless night, a brave soul ventured forth, listening to the birch tree's branches as they parted, revealing the ghostly woman. Her eyes held centuries of sorrow and her lips moved silently. The woman's breath, icy as death, brushed against his ear. Then the Lady in White vanished, her laughter echoing through the night.

From then on, the townsfolk avoided the birch tree and the ghost it harbored. The whispers, though, persisted, carried by the wind, weaving tales. The birch may be at rest now but is waiting to awaken once more. Beware not to leave a mark upon it and free bad spirits into our world.

CHAPTER 13: DEATH RITES IN FALL BROOK

As there was life in Fall Brook, so there was death. Early undertakers tended to work as builders and made furniture or cabinets. Later, they expanded into coffin making. There were two distinct differences between a coffin and a casket. Coffins were tapered at the head and foot and had a removable lid. Caskets, though, were rectangular and contained a hinged lid. Only prominent families could afford the latter.

At times of death in Fall Brook, the family would first obtain a death certificate from a doctor. Then the local "layer outer," usually a woman, would attend to the needs of the deceased and the bereaved. After she performed her duties, the priest or minister was called to perform last rites.

Finally, the undertaker came to take measurements for the coffin. He built it as quickly as possible from sanded and polished hardwood. It was then sealed inside with wax.

It was the custom for the community's young folk to "sit up" with the dead. In those days, a body wasn't embalmed, so the "sitters" placed dampened cloths on the hands and face of the deceased. That kept the skin from darkening until the day of the funeral.

Once the coffin was built, the undertaker delivered it to the mourning family. The dearly departed was then dressed in his or her best suit or night dress and placed inside. The dead person was displayed in the parlor for three to four days while the church and family planned the funeral arrangements. Sweet smelling flowers were placed around the room to absorb bad odors, and the undertaker would visit often to check on any unpleasantness.

The livery stable provided the horse-drawn hearse for the trip to Fall Brook Cemetery. The blacksmith was often the respected driver. After all, he had forged the horseshoes and nails for the coffin and built the wagon wheels that made the deceased's final journey possible.

The first burial at Fall Brook Cemetery was that of G.A. Beckus, brother of Mrs. Humphries Brewer. He died in February of 1864 after being one of the town's first civil engineers and coal explorers. Others soon followed, victims of smallpox and typhoid fever outbreaks. Silas Cleveland was given the job of posting quarantine signs when such diseases struck the village.

The *Steuben Farmers' Advocate* ran regular obituaries of those who died in Fall Brook. In

1875, the newspaper reported that a young brakeman named John Smith was crushed by a train near the depot. He was trying to uncouple some cars when he slipped and fell under the wheels. The accident was described as "one of the most shocking and heart-rending" that ever occurred in the town. Another terrible incident happened in 1884 when a boiler exploded at the saw mill, killing four men and injuring several others.

In 1886, the obit of Thomas Jones ran in the *Farmers' Advocate*. He was a native of Wales and came to America during the War of 1812. He settled in Fall Brook in 1856 and worked as a miner until he retired at the age of ninety. The father of twelve children, he was a "remarkable example of longevity."

The following year, Mrs. Mary Jones died at her home after a long illness. She was the wife of William Jones, a prominent citizen and merchant. The newspaper praised her as "a kind and affectionate wife and mother."

One of the oldest and most respected residents died in 1894. He was John C. Brown, a native of England. Engaged in the coal business, he was justice of the peace, a school trustee, and a Mason, to boot. His achievements filled up a lengthy column in the *Steuben Farmers' Advocate*.

CHAPTER 14: FALL BROOK CEMETERY

As I stood in the dark entrance of Fall Brook Cemetery, I credited my anxiousness to an overactive imagination. Yet, the feeling persisted when I moved deeper into the grounds. The shadows thickened, and the air grew colder, too. I shivered after noting how the moonlight pooled around a weathered stone adorned with the name Robert Russell.

I stepped closer, drawn to Robert's resting place. Then, from the corner of my eye, I saw the movement of a figure obscured by gloom. I heard someone approach me but turned and found nobody there.

"Who are you?" I whispered, my breath visible in the night air.

The figure drew nearer, and I saw a derby hat, a brown jacket, and a pale face filled with questions. He glowed ethereally, seeking solace in the moon's embrace.

"A man. A writer," he murmured, his voice like the rustle of leaves. "Tell my story. Please."

"Why?" I asked, my pen trembling as I scribbled notes. "Why me?"

"Because you listen. Because you feel the weight of forgotten lives. Tell them we exist beyond the grave. That our stories linger in the moonlight."

And so I penned Robert's tale—the love lost, the promises broken, the ache that transcended death. As I finished, the figure faded, leaving only the whispered echo of gratitude.

I had felt the existence of other ghosts who exist outside the cemetery, as well. They hovered along Hemlock Lane on Welch Mountain where the eerie remains of the old railroad bed are still seen. The whistles of phantom trains echo there as does the voice of John Magee who barks out commands to his spectral workers.

A little farther to the right is the entrance of an old mine shaft guarded by an energy named Andrew. Trust me, he guards it well! Equally active is the Civil War soldier in the cemetery itself. He beats his drum when prompted by period music and marches smartly along.

Before entering the gates of the graveyard, though, permission must be asked of the stately lady who guards them. Those who gain admittance must have good intentions and promise not to do mischief. A small offering of flowers will guarantee safe passage. An opening prayer should always be said, as well.

To the right, in the woods, the spirit of a woman named Ann mourns the loss of her husband. She was but twenty-four years old and already a widow. Standing in her grave clothes, she murmurs and makes gestures. "My husband," she chokes. "My husband, Thomas."

I was afraid at first when she called out to me, because she was beckoning me into the woods. Now, I know she meant no harm. When she was alive, there was no forest where she stood.

In the back right hand corner of the cemetery, a family of five are buried, and there are children all around. I'm always kind to two-year-old Sadie who tugs on my clothes and tries to hold my hand. I never brush her away to make her cry. She is so sweet and loves the toys I leave her.

Mary is a lady who revealed my past life to me. Her face appears on the headstone of a little boy named John. Although he is one of her family, his grave is not her resting place. Sadly, she will not always show herself.

The Swedish man who says, "Guten tag," or "Good morning," makes himself known in numerous ways. He died of a hematoma during a holiday, and his records are on file.

Before leaving Fall Brook, I always ask that spirits not follow me home. Sometimes, they simply won't listen. Such was the case of Robert Russell, who was born on April 12, 1834 and died on November 12, 1905.

I first became aware of Robert when he came to live with me at my house on Welch

Mountain. To attract my attention, he doffed his hat three times like Gene Kelly, the well-known dancer and actor. It was then that I realized my friends and I had talked about the people buried in the cemetery but had forgotten to mention the Irish. Robert was not a bothersome energy. He was happy when he returned to his gravesite and my friend's planted potatoes for him and took him shamrocks.

A terrifying energy attached itself to me next when I least expected it. I was visiting the site of my favorite spirit, Mary, when I noticed her stone was tipped over to the ground. I wanted to lift it back in place, but it was too heavy even for two people. As I looked at the headstone, I felt like I could not move from it, because my feet were like cement blocks. My energy also began to shift and my hair and features changed. Something was happening that I couldn't explain. Even my friends noticed it but didn't say anything that day.

Soon, my attitude became one of anger and panic. Then night visits began from the most frightening energy that I've ever been in contact with. He looked a bit like Uncle Fester from the Addams family and appeared nightly to rage and cackle. His antics continued for over a week until he really wore me down.

I finally had enough of his haunting and bravely bid him to go back to the cemetery. After I cleansed my house and prayed, I said I would lead him by the hand to where he belonged. I used all my energy and the energy of others to send the elemental away.

The thing I learned most about Fall Brook from my many visits there is that it's a portal to the past where the living and departed intersect. Contrary to what most people believe about ghosts, they may be seen as daytime apparitions as well as nighttime specters. Whenever I feel a ghostly presence, I stand still and see what it is trying to say to me. I believe most ghosts want to interact with us on a positive level. The dead are interred in a north-south line in this burial place while in most cemeteries people are buried from east to west. Maybe that's why so many restless spirits flit among the rising caskets and blighted tombstones like the many dragonflies that swarm the grounds.

CHAPTER 15: EPILOGUE

Fall Brook Cemetery is located off a state forest road in Ward Township, Tioga County, Pennsylvania. Its fallen and broken gravestones bear witness to the passage of time as no burials have occurred here for over a century. The graveyard rests in quiet abandonment with its secrets buried among the departed. The names of the lives once lived are now etched in moss-covered stone. Visitors who venture here may feel the weight of history.

Fall Brook Cemetery, now a silent sentinel, cradles the memories of those who danced at harvest festivals, who whispered secrets under moonlit skies, and who weathered many storms. Their stories are like the gnarled roots of apple trees intertwined with the very soil that cradles them.

And so, in my humble endeavor to honor these souls, I compile their names as a litany of remembrance. I pen their stories, not as mere dates and inscriptions, but as echoes of love and loss. For they are more than names etched in granite; they are the heartbeat of the community that once thrived here.

In this abandoned town, where the wind rustles through forgotten doorways and wildflowers reclaim the streets, I offer my tribute. With each keystroke, I resurrect their voices, weaving them into the fabric of my book. Their legacy, obscured by time, deserves recognition— a whispered promise that they shall not fade into oblivion.

And so, dear reader, as you scan the pages of my work, know that it is not just ink on paper. It's a bridge across centuries, a bridge that spans the gap between the living and the departed. For in honoring their memory, we honor our shared humanity—a beautiful tapestry that transcends the boundaries of time and place.

"Here lies our past," the gravestones murmur. "Remember us:"

Fall Brook Cemetery

I.A.

Agnes Brown Adam

Alexander Pollock Adam

Hiram Allen

Jinnet M. Allen

John P. Allen

Robert J. Allen

Brigitta Anderson

Isabelle Anderson

James Asherman, Jr.

C.R.B.

Isabelle B.

Margret Barr

G.A. Beckus

James Berwick

John Berwick

Margaret Berwick

William Berwick

Alvin V. Bland

Damon Bland

Lincoln Bland

William Bland

George Bliss

John Bodin

Anna M. Bolt

Ann Bolt

Daniel Bolt

Francis L. Bolt

John Bolt

Margret Stemoviht Bolt

Marshall Bolt

William Bolt

Esther Bolton

Humphries Brewer

Eliza Brice

George Broadbent

Jane Broadbent

Agnes S. Brown

Alexander Brown

Christina Brown

Eliza Brown

Janet Brownlie

Alexander Bruce, Jr.

Christina Bruce

James W. Bruce

Ann Burton

Dorothy A. Burton

Infant son Burton

Thomas Burton

James C (?)

P.C.

Archable Chambers

Archable Alexander Chambers

James Chambers

Mary Chambers

Amy Knowles Cook

George Cook

George Coon

Enoch Cox

Theopailas Cox

Edward Forrest Cummings

Agnes Cunningham

William Cunningham

Catherine Davis

David J. Davis

Gwenllian Davis

Thomas Davis

William Davis

William M. Davis

Susan DeWalt

Infants Dick

John L. Dick

Walter Dick

Jeanett Dryburg

E.E.

Benjamin Eildings

George Estep

Mary Estep

A.F.

Eliza Flick

Andrew N. Forsyth

Mrs. Alfred William Furman

Mary Jane Gaffney

Sarah J. Gaffney

Ann Gardiner

Thomas Edward Gardiner

Ann Gough

Elizabeth Griffin

James Griffin

Samuel Grant

William Grant

A.E.H.

James Haddow

Marian Haddow

Anna D. Hagstron

William Sambrook Hall

William H. Hambley

Richard Harrison

John l. Hatherill

Jennie Hay

Robert Hay

John Henry

Mary Jane Henry

Sarah A. Henry

James Heron

Thomas D. Hind

Angus Holt

William Holt

William T. Holt

Alexander Hunter

A.J.

Joseph James

Anna Johnson

Anna P. Johnson

Hanning Johnson

Hilma M. Johnson

Abrather Jones

Catherine "Cassie" Jones

Catherine Pearson "Katie" Jones

Fredrick T. Jones

George Jones

James F. Jones

James Thomas Jones

Stuart Jones

Charles Henry Keefer

Sarah J. Kennedy

Mary A. Kirk

Elizabeth Kitson

Sarah J. Kitson

William Kitson

John Lewis

Mary Lewis

Stanley Y. Lyon

A.M.

Nicol McNicol

Emily Meredith

Thomas Moorry

Agnes Nicol Muir

Robert Muir

Janet Nicol

William Nicol

Beckus Orton

Gustavus E. Orton

Lemuel J. Owen

WP

Isabelle M. Patterson

Jane Ellen Payne

Pehr Pehrson

Pettronilla Pehrson

Henry Perry

Thomas Perry

Elizabeth Pollock

Mary Powell

William Poxon

Robert Pryde

John Reid

J. S. Renwicks

Thomas Renwicks

William Roberts

Martha Rowley

Anna A. Russell

Annie Forbes Russell

Janet Russell

John Russell

Robert Russell

(?) Shearer

Jeanette Shearer

Robert Shearer

Matilda Shepard

Sadie Simpson

Tommy Smith

Elsie Spencer

Earl Stevens

Elnora Stevens

Charles Strange

William Thomas

James W.

T.W.

Helen Walker

Janeourley Walker

John Walker

John Wardrop

Infant Watson

John Watson

Ethel Wells

Mary Wells

Ann Whitehouse

Minerva Whiting

Ann Williams

Elizabeth Jane Williams

Humphrey Williams

M. Williams

Selma Williams

Sophia Williams

Thomas Williams

Thomas Wilson

Fannie E. Wilson

Joseph Wilson

Caroline Unknown

Ellen Unknown

Margaret Unknown

Unknown

Unfortunately, some names and markers at the Fall Brook Cemetery have been lost to time and the elements, so not every soul buried there is accounted for. That includes many little ones whose lives were claimed during the smallpox epidemic that raged through the borough during the winter of 1871-1872. Remember these children and say a prayer for them.

ABOUT THE AUTHOR

Shirley M. Welch is a lifetime resident of Covington, Pennsylvania who describes herself as "a woman of resilience, a lover of history, and a believer in what lies beyond." Now, she can add "author" to her resume.

Shirley has always been fascinated with the paranormal and its ghosts, spirits, and stay-behinds. She believes that ghosts are lingering souls who defy space and time.

From when she was a small child, Welch was drawn to Fall Brook Cemetery. She began by finding the well-hidden graveyard and then spent years unearthing its secrets and history. In her book, she attempts to resurrect the forgotten town and its miners, shopkeepers, and dusky phantoms.